This Book Belongs To:

NAME	
ADDRESS	
PHONE NUMBER	
EMAIL	

Copyright © Teresa Rother
All rights reserved. No part of this publication may be reproduced, distributed, or transmitted in any form or by any means, including photocopy, recording, or other electronic or mechanical methods.

Dedication

This Guest Book is dedicated to all the people who want to track and record visitor information and comments about their stay.

You are my inspiration for producing this book and I'm honored to be a part of your record-keeping and organization.

How to Use This Book

This Guest Book will help you by accurately recording guest information.

Here are examples of information for you to fill in and write the details of your logbook.

Fill in the following information:

1. Guest Name
2. Contact Number
3. Traveled From
4. Date Departed
5. Weather
6. Favorite Thing About The Property
7. Favorite Memories From Your Stay
8. Activities I Enjoyed The Most
9. Places I Would Recommend
10. Special Message To The Host

Guest Book

GUEST NAME		CONTACT NUMBER	
DATE ARRIVED		DATE DEPARTED	
TRAVELING FROM			
WEATHER			

MY FAVORITE THING ABOUT THE PROPERTY

MY FAVORITE MEMORY FROM THE STAY	ACTIVITIES I ENJOYED THE MOST

PLACES I WOULD RECOMMEND (RESTAURANTS, SHOPPING, ENTERTAINMENT, ETC.)

SPECIAL MESSAGE TO THE HOST

Guest Book

GUEST NAME		CONTACT NUMBER	
DATE ARRIVED		DATE DEPARTED	
TRAVELING FROM			
WEATHER			

MY FAVORITE THING ABOUT THE PROPERTY

MY FAVORITE MEMORY FROM THE STAY	ACTIVITIES I ENJOYED THE MOST

PLACES I WOULD RECOMMEND (RESTAURANTS, SHOPPING, ENTERTAINMENT, ETC.)

SPECIAL MESSAGE TO THE HOST

Guest Book

GUEST NAME		CONTACT NUMBER	
DATE ARRIVED		DATE DEPARTED	
TRAVELING FROM			
WEATHER			

MY FAVORITE THING ABOUT THE PROPERTY

MY FAVORITE MEMORY FROM THE STAY	ACTIVITIES I ENJOYED THE MOST

PLACES I WOULD RECOMMEND
(RESTAURANTS, SHOPPING, ENTERTAINMENT, ETC.)

SPECIAL MESSAGE TO THE HOST

Guest Book

GUEST NAME		CONTACT NUMBER	
DATE ARRIVED		DATE DEPARTED	
TRAVELING FROM			
WEATHER			

MY FAVORITE THING ABOUT THE PROPERTY

MY FAVORITE MEMORY FROM THE STAY	ACTIVITIES I ENJOYED THE MOST

PLACES I WOULD RECOMMEND (RESTAURANTS, SHOPPING, ENTERTAINMENT, ETC.)

SPECIAL MESSAGE TO THE HOST

Guest Book

GUEST NAME		CONTACT NUMBER	
DATE ARRIVED		DATE DEPARTED	
TRAVELING FROM			
WEATHER			

MY FAVORITE THING ABOUT THE PROPERTY

MY FAVORITE MEMORY FROM THE STAY	ACTIVITIES I ENJOYED THE MOST

| PLACES I WOULD RECOMMEND |
(RESTAURANTS, SHOPPING, ENTERTAINMENT, ETC.)

SPECIAL MESSAGE TO THE HOST

Guest Book

GUEST NAME		CONTACT NUMBER	
DATE ARRIVED		DATE DEPARTED	
TRAVELING FROM			
WEATHER			

MY FAVORITE THING ABOUT THE PROPERTY

MY FAVORITE MEMORY FROM THE STAY	ACTIVITIES I ENJOYED THE MOST

PLACES I WOULD RECOMMEND
(RESTAURANTS, SHOPPING, ENTERTAINMENT, ETC.)

SPECIAL MESSAGE TO THE HOST

Guest Book

GUEST NAME		CONTACT NUMBER	
DATE ARRIVED		DATE DEPARTED	
TRAVELING FROM			
WEATHER			

MY FAVORITE THING ABOUT THE PROPERTY

MY FAVORITE MEMORY FROM THE STAY	ACTIVITIES I ENJOYED THE MOST

PLACES I WOULD RECOMMEND
(RESTAURANTS, SHOPPING, ENTERTAINMENT, ETC.)

SPECIAL MESSAGE TO THE HOST

Guest Book

GUEST NAME		CONTACT NUMBER	
DATE ARRIVED		DATE DEPARTED	
TRAVELING FROM			
WEATHER			

MY FAVORITE THING ABOUT THE PROPERTY

MY FAVORITE MEMORY FROM THE STAY	ACTIVITIES I ENJOYED THE MOST

| PLACES I WOULD RECOMMEND |
(RESTAURANTS, SHOPPING, ENTERTAINMENT, ETC.)

SPECIAL MESSAGE TO THE HOST

Guest Book

GUEST NAME		CONTACT NUMBER	
DATE ARRIVED		DATE DEPARTED	
TRAVELING FROM			
WEATHER			

MY FAVORITE THING ABOUT THE PROPERTY

MY FAVORITE MEMORY FROM THE STAY	ACTIVITIES I ENJOYED THE MOST

| PLACES I WOULD RECOMMEND |
(RESTAURANTS, SHOPPING, ENTERTAINMENT, ETC.)

SPECIAL MESSAGE TO THE HOST

Guest Book

GUEST NAME		CONTACT NUMBER	
DATE ARRIVED		DATE DEPARTED	
TRAVELING FROM			
WEATHER			

MY FAVORITE THING ABOUT THE PROPERTY

MY FAVORITE MEMORY FROM THE STAY	ACTIVITIES I ENJOYED THE MOST

PLACES I WOULD RECOMMEND (RESTAURANTS, SHOPPING, ENTERTAINMENT, ETC.)

SPECIAL MESSAGE TO THE HOST

Guest Book

GUEST NAME		CONTACT NUMBER	
DATE ARRIVED		DATE DEPARTED	
TRAVELING FROM			
WEATHER			

MY FAVORITE THING ABOUT THE PROPERTY

MY FAVORITE MEMORY FROM THE STAY	ACTIVITIES I ENJOYED THE MOST

PLACES I WOULD RECOMMEND
(RESTAURANTS, SHOPPING, ENTERTAINMENT, ETC.)

SPECIAL MESSAGE TO THE HOST

Guest Book

GUEST NAME		CONTACT NUMBER	
DATE ARRIVED		DATE DEPARTED	
TRAVELING FROM			
WEATHER			

MY FAVORITE THING ABOUT THE PROPERTY

MY FAVORITE MEMORY FROM THE STAY	ACTIVITIES I ENJOYED THE MOST

| PLACES I WOULD RECOMMEND |
(RESTAURANTS, SHOPPING, ENTERTAINMENT, ETC.)

SPECIAL MESSAGE TO THE HOST

Guest Book

GUEST NAME		CONTACT NUMBER	
DATE ARRIVED		DATE DEPARTED	
TRAVELING FROM			
WEATHER			

MY FAVORITE THING ABOUT THE PROPERTY

MY FAVORITE MEMORY FROM THE STAY	ACTIVITIES I ENJOYED THE MOST

PLACES I WOULD RECOMMEND (RESTAURANTS, SHOPPING, ENTERTAINMENT, ETC.)

SPECIAL MESSAGE TO THE HOST

Guest Book

GUEST NAME		CONTACT NUMBER	
DATE ARRIVED		DATE DEPARTED	
TRAVELING FROM			
WEATHER			

MY FAVORITE THING ABOUT THE PROPERTY

MY FAVORITE MEMORY FROM THE STAY	ACTIVITIES I ENJOYED THE MOST

| PLACES I WOULD RECOMMEND |
(RESTAURANTS, SHOPPING, ENTERTAINMENT, ETC.)

SPECIAL MESSAGE TO THE HOST

Guest Book

GUEST NAME		CONTACT NUMBER	
DATE ARRIVED		DATE DEPARTED	
TRAVELING FROM			
WEATHER			

MY FAVORITE THING ABOUT THE PROPERTY

MY FAVORITE MEMORY FROM THE STAY	ACTIVITIES I ENJOYED THE MOST

PLACES I WOULD RECOMMEND
(RESTAURANTS, SHOPPING, ENTERTAINMENT, ETC.)

SPECIAL MESSAGE TO THE HOST

Guest Book

GUEST NAME		CONTACT NUMBER	
DATE ARRIVED		DATE DEPARTED	
TRAVELING FROM			
WEATHER			

MY FAVORITE THING ABOUT THE PROPERTY

MY FAVORITE MEMORY FROM THE STAY	ACTIVITIES I ENJOYED THE MOST

PLACES I WOULD RECOMMEND
(RESTAURANTS, SHOPPING, ENTERTAINMENT, ETC.)

SPECIAL MESSAGE TO THE HOST

Guest Book

GUEST NAME		CONTACT NUMBER	
DATE ARRIVED		DATE DEPARTED	
TRAVELING FROM			
WEATHER			

MY FAVORITE THING ABOUT THE PROPERTY

MY FAVORITE MEMORY FROM THE STAY	ACTIVITIES I ENJOYED THE MOST

PLACES I WOULD RECOMMEND
(RESTAURANTS, SHOPPING, ENTERTAINMENT, ETC.)

SPECIAL MESSAGE TO THE HOST

Guest Book

GUEST NAME		CONTACT NUMBER	
DATE ARRIVED		DATE DEPARTED	
TRAVELING FROM			
WEATHER			

MY FAVORITE THING ABOUT THE PROPERTY

MY FAVORITE MEMORY FROM THE STAY	ACTIVITIES I ENJOYED THE MOST

PLACES I WOULD RECOMMEND (RESTAURANTS, SHOPPING, ENTERTAINMENT, ETC.)

SPECIAL MESSAGE TO THE HOST

Guest Book

GUEST NAME		CONTACT NUMBER	
DATE ARRIVED		DATE DEPARTED	
TRAVELING FROM			
WEATHER			

MY FAVORITE THING ABOUT THE PROPERTY

MY FAVORITE MEMORY FROM THE STAY	ACTIVITIES I ENJOYED THE MOST

PLACES I WOULD RECOMMEND
(RESTAURANTS, SHOPPING, ENTERTAINMENT, ETC.)

SPECIAL MESSAGE TO THE HOST

Guest Book

GUEST NAME		CONTACT NUMBER	
DATE ARRIVED		DATE DEPARTED	
TRAVELING FROM			
WEATHER			

MY FAVORITE THING ABOUT THE PROPERTY

MY FAVORITE MEMORY FROM THE STAY	ACTIVITIES I ENJOYED THE MOST

| PLACES I WOULD RECOMMEND |
(RESTAURANTS, SHOPPING, ENTERTAINMENT, ETC.)

SPECIAL MESSAGE TO THE HOST

Guest Book

GUEST NAME		CONTACT NUMBER	
DATE ARRIVED		DATE DEPARTED	
TRAVELING FROM			
WEATHER			

MY FAVORITE THING ABOUT THE PROPERTY

MY FAVORITE MEMORY FROM THE STAY	ACTIVITIES I ENJOYED THE MOST

| PLACES I WOULD RECOMMEND |
(RESTAURANTS, SHOPPING, ENTERTAINMENT, ETC.)

SPECIAL MESSAGE TO THE HOST

Guest Book

GUEST NAME		CONTACT NUMBER	
DATE ARRIVED		DATE DEPARTED	
TRAVELING FROM			
WEATHER			

MY FAVORITE THING ABOUT THE PROPERTY

MY FAVORITE MEMORY FROM THE STAY	ACTIVITIES I ENJOYED THE MOST

PLACES I WOULD RECOMMEND (RESTAURANTS, SHOPPING, ENTERTAINMENT, ETC.)

SPECIAL MESSAGE TO THE HOST

Guest Book

GUEST NAME		CONTACT NUMBER	
DATE ARRIVED		DATE DEPARTED	
TRAVELING FROM			
WEATHER			

MY FAVORITE THING ABOUT THE PROPERTY

MY FAVORITE MEMORY FROM THE STAY	ACTIVITIES I ENJOYED THE MOST

PLACES I WOULD RECOMMEND
(RESTAURANTS, SHOPPING, ENTERTAINMENT, ETC.)

SPECIAL MESSAGE TO THE HOST

Guest Book

GUEST NAME		CONTACT NUMBER	
DATE ARRIVED		DATE DEPARTED	
TRAVELING FROM			
WEATHER			

MY FAVORITE THING ABOUT THE PROPERTY

MY FAVORITE MEMORY FROM THE STAY	ACTIVITIES I ENJOYED THE MOST

PLACES I WOULD RECOMMEND
(RESTAURANTS, SHOPPING, ENTERTAINMENT, ETC.)

SPECIAL MESSAGE TO THE HOST

Guest Book

GUEST NAME		CONTACT NUMBER	
DATE ARRIVED		DATE DEPARTED	
TRAVELING FROM			
WEATHER			

MY FAVORITE THING ABOUT THE PROPERTY

MY FAVORITE MEMORY FROM THE STAY	ACTIVITIES I ENJOYED THE MOST

PLACES I WOULD RECOMMEND
(RESTAURANTS, SHOPPING, ENTERTAINMENT, ETC.)

SPECIAL MESSAGE TO THE HOST

Guest Book

GUEST NAME		CONTACT NUMBER	
DATE ARRIVED		DATE DEPARTED	
TRAVELING FROM			
WEATHER			

MY FAVORITE THING ABOUT THE PROPERTY

MY FAVORITE MEMORY FROM THE STAY	ACTIVITIES I ENJOYED THE MOST

PLACES I WOULD RECOMMEND (RESTAURANTS, SHOPPING, ENTERTAINMENT, ETC.)

SPECIAL MESSAGE TO THE HOST

Guest Book

GUEST NAME		CONTACT NUMBER	
DATE ARRIVED		DATE DEPARTED	
TRAVELING FROM			
WEATHER			

MY FAVORITE THING ABOUT THE PROPERTY

MY FAVORITE MEMORY FROM THE STAY	ACTIVITIES I ENJOYED THE MOST

PLACES I WOULD RECOMMEND
(RESTAURANTS, SHOPPING, ENTERTAINMENT, ETC.)

SPECIAL MESSAGE TO THE HOST

Guest Book

GUEST NAME		CONTACT NUMBER	
DATE ARRIVED		DATE DEPARTED	
TRAVELING FROM			
WEATHER			

MY FAVORITE THING ABOUT THE PROPERTY

MY FAVORITE MEMORY FROM THE STAY	ACTIVITIES I ENJOYED THE MOST

| PLACES I WOULD RECOMMEND |
(RESTAURANTS, SHOPPING, ENTERTAINMENT, ETC.)

SPECIAL MESSAGE TO THE HOST

Guest Book

GUEST NAME		CONTACT NUMBER	
DATE ARRIVED		DATE DEPARTED	
TRAVELING FROM			
WEATHER			

MY FAVORITE THING ABOUT THE PROPERTY

MY FAVORITE MEMORY FROM THE STAY	ACTIVITIES I ENJOYED THE MOST

PLACES I WOULD RECOMMEND
(RESTAURANTS, SHOPPING, ENTERTAINMENT, ETC.)

SPECIAL MESSAGE TO THE HOST

Guest Book

GUEST NAME		CONTACT NUMBER	
DATE ARRIVED		DATE DEPARTED	
TRAVELING FROM			
WEATHER			

MY FAVORITE THING ABOUT THE PROPERTY

MY FAVORITE MEMORY FROM THE STAY	ACTIVITIES I ENJOYED THE MOST

PLACES I WOULD RECOMMEND (RESTAURANTS, SHOPPING, ENTERTAINMENT, ETC.)

SPECIAL MESSAGE TO THE HOST

Guest Book

GUEST NAME		CONTACT NUMBER	
DATE ARRIVED		DATE DEPARTED	
TRAVELING FROM			
WEATHER			

MY FAVORITE THING ABOUT THE PROPERTY

MY FAVORITE MEMORY FROM THE STAY	ACTIVITIES I ENJOYED THE MOST

PLACES I WOULD RECOMMEND
(RESTAURANTS, SHOPPING, ENTERTAINMENT, ETC.)

SPECIAL MESSAGE TO THE HOST

Guest Book

GUEST NAME		CONTACT NUMBER	
DATE ARRIVED		DATE DEPARTED	
TRAVELING FROM			
WEATHER			

MY FAVORITE THING ABOUT THE PROPERTY

MY FAVORITE MEMORY FROM THE STAY	ACTIVITIES I ENJOYED THE MOST

PLACES I WOULD RECOMMEND (RESTAURANTS, SHOPPING, ENTERTAINMENT, ETC.)

SPECIAL MESSAGE TO THE HOST

Guest Book

GUEST NAME		CONTACT NUMBER	
DATE ARRIVED		DATE DEPARTED	
TRAVELING FROM			
WEATHER			

MY FAVORITE THING ABOUT THE PROPERTY

MY FAVORITE MEMORY FROM THE STAY	ACTIVITIES I ENJOYED THE MOST

PLACES I WOULD RECOMMEND
(RESTAURANTS, SHOPPING, ENTERTAINMENT, ETC.)

SPECIAL MESSAGE TO THE HOST

Guest Book

GUEST NAME		CONTACT NUMBER	
DATE ARRIVED		DATE DEPARTED	
TRAVELING FROM			
WEATHER			

MY FAVORITE THING ABOUT THE PROPERTY

MY FAVORITE MEMORY FROM THE STAY	ACTIVITIES I ENJOYED THE MOST

| PLACES I WOULD RECOMMEND |
(RESTAURANTS, SHOPPING, ENTERTAINMENT, ETC.)

SPECIAL MESSAGE TO THE HOST

Guest Book

GUEST NAME		CONTACT NUMBER	
DATE ARRIVED		DATE DEPARTED	
TRAVELING FROM			
WEATHER			

MY FAVORITE THING ABOUT THE PROPERTY

MY FAVORITE MEMORY FROM THE STAY	ACTIVITIES I ENJOYED THE MOST

PLACES I WOULD RECOMMEND
(RESTAURANTS, SHOPPING, ENTERTAINMENT, ETC.)

SPECIAL MESSAGE TO THE HOST

Guest Book

GUEST NAME		CONTACT NUMBER	
DATE ARRIVED		DATE DEPARTED	
TRAVELING FROM			
WEATHER			

MY FAVORITE THING ABOUT THE PROPERTY

MY FAVORITE MEMORY FROM THE STAY	ACTIVITIES I ENJOYED THE MOST

PLACES I WOULD RECOMMEND
(RESTAURANTS, SHOPPING, ENTERTAINMENT, ETC.)

SPECIAL MESSAGE TO THE HOST

Guest Book

GUEST NAME		CONTACT NUMBER	
DATE ARRIVED		DATE DEPARTED	
TRAVELING FROM			
WEATHER			

MY FAVORITE THING ABOUT THE PROPERTY

MY FAVORITE MEMORY FROM THE STAY	ACTIVITIES I ENJOYED THE MOST

PLACES I WOULD RECOMMEND
(RESTAURANTS, SHOPPING, ENTERTAINMENT, ETC.)

SPECIAL MESSAGE TO THE HOST

Guest Book

GUEST NAME		CONTACT NUMBER	
DATE ARRIVED		DATE DEPARTED	
TRAVELING FROM			
WEATHER			

MY FAVORITE THING ABOUT THE PROPERTY

MY FAVORITE MEMORY FROM THE STAY	ACTIVITIES I ENJOYED THE MOST

PLACES I WOULD RECOMMEND (RESTAURANTS, SHOPPING, ENTERTAINMENT, ETC.)

SPECIAL MESSAGE TO THE HOST

Guest Book

GUEST NAME		CONTACT NUMBER	
DATE ARRIVED		DATE DEPARTED	
TRAVELING FROM			
WEATHER			

MY FAVORITE THING ABOUT THE PROPERTY

MY FAVORITE MEMORY FROM THE STAY	ACTIVITIES I ENJOYED THE MOST

PLACES I WOULD RECOMMEND
(RESTAURANTS, SHOPPING, ENTERTAINMENT, ETC.)

SPECIAL MESSAGE TO THE HOST

Guest Book

GUEST NAME		CONTACT NUMBER	
DATE ARRIVED		DATE DEPARTED	
TRAVELING FROM			
WEATHER			

MY FAVORITE THING ABOUT THE PROPERTY

MY FAVORITE MEMORY FROM THE STAY	ACTIVITIES I ENJOYED THE MOST

PLACES I WOULD RECOMMEND (RESTAURANTS, SHOPPING, ENTERTAINMENT, ETC.)

SPECIAL MESSAGE TO THE HOST

Guest Book

GUEST NAME		CONTACT NUMBER	
DATE ARRIVED		DATE DEPARTED	
TRAVELING FROM			
WEATHER			

MY FAVORITE THING ABOUT THE PROPERTY

MY FAVORITE MEMORY FROM THE STAY	ACTIVITIES I ENJOYED THE MOST

PLACES I WOULD RECOMMEND
(RESTAURANTS, SHOPPING, ENTERTAINMENT, ETC.)

SPECIAL MESSAGE TO THE HOST

Guest Book

GUEST NAME		CONTACT NUMBER	
DATE ARRIVED		DATE DEPARTED	
TRAVELING FROM			
WEATHER			

MY FAVORITE THING ABOUT THE PROPERTY

MY FAVORITE MEMORY FROM THE STAY	ACTIVITIES I ENJOYED THE MOST

| PLACES I WOULD RECOMMEND |
(RESTAURANTS, SHOPPING, ENTERTAINMENT, ETC.)

SPECIAL MESSAGE TO THE HOST

Guest Book

GUEST NAME		CONTACT NUMBER	
DATE ARRIVED		DATE DEPARTED	
TRAVELING FROM			
WEATHER			

MY FAVORITE THING ABOUT THE PROPERTY

MY FAVORITE MEMORY FROM THE STAY	ACTIVITIES I ENJOYED THE MOST

PLACES I WOULD RECOMMEND (RESTAURANTS, SHOPPING, ENTERTAINMENT, ETC.)

SPECIAL MESSAGE TO THE HOST

Guest Book

GUEST NAME		CONTACT NUMBER	
DATE ARRIVED		DATE DEPARTED	
TRAVELING FROM			
WEATHER			

MY FAVORITE THING ABOUT THE PROPERTY

MY FAVORITE MEMORY FROM THE STAY	ACTIVITIES I ENJOYED THE MOST

PLACES I WOULD RECOMMEND (RESTAURANTS, SHOPPING, ENTERTAINMENT, ETC.)

SPECIAL MESSAGE TO THE HOST

Guest Book

GUEST NAME		CONTACT NUMBER	
DATE ARRIVED		DATE DEPARTED	
TRAVELING FROM			
WEATHER			

MY FAVORITE THING ABOUT THE PROPERTY

MY FAVORITE MEMORY FROM THE STAY	ACTIVITIES I ENJOYED THE MOST

PLACES I WOULD RECOMMEND
(RESTAURANTS, SHOPPING, ENTERTAINMENT, ETC.)

SPECIAL MESSAGE TO THE HOST

Guest Book

GUEST NAME		CONTACT NUMBER	
DATE ARRIVED		DATE DEPARTED	
TRAVELING FROM			
WEATHER			

MY FAVORITE THING ABOUT THE PROPERTY

MY FAVORITE MEMORY FROM THE STAY	ACTIVITIES I ENJOYED THE MOST

PLACES I WOULD RECOMMEND
(RESTAURANTS, SHOPPING, ENTERTAINMENT, ETC.)

SPECIAL MESSAGE TO THE HOST

Guest Book

GUEST NAME		CONTACT NUMBER	
DATE ARRIVED		DATE DEPARTED	
TRAVELING FROM			
WEATHER			

MY FAVORITE THING ABOUT THE PROPERTY

MY FAVORITE MEMORY FROM THE STAY	ACTIVITIES I ENJOYED THE MOST

| PLACES I WOULD RECOMMEND |
(RESTAURANTS, SHOPPING, ENTERTAINMENT, ETC.)

SPECIAL MESSAGE TO THE HOST

Guest Book

GUEST NAME		CONTACT NUMBER	
DATE ARRIVED		DATE DEPARTED	
TRAVELING FROM			
WEATHER			

MY FAVORITE THING ABOUT THE PROPERTY

MY FAVORITE MEMORY FROM THE STAY	ACTIVITIES I ENJOYED THE MOST

| PLACES I WOULD RECOMMEND |
(RESTAURANTS, SHOPPING, ENTERTAINMENT, ETC.)

SPECIAL MESSAGE TO THE HOST

Guest Book

GUEST NAME		CONTACT NUMBER	
DATE ARRIVED		DATE DEPARTED	
TRAVELING FROM			
WEATHER			

MY FAVORITE THING ABOUT THE PROPERTY

MY FAVORITE MEMORY FROM THE STAY	ACTIVITIES I ENJOYED THE MOST

| PLACES I WOULD RECOMMEND |
(RESTAURANTS, SHOPPING, ENTERTAINMENT, ETC.)

SPECIAL MESSAGE TO THE HOST

Guest Book

GUEST NAME		CONTACT NUMBER	
DATE ARRIVED		DATE DEPARTED	
TRAVELING FROM			
WEATHER			

MY FAVORITE THING ABOUT THE PROPERTY

MY FAVORITE MEMORY FROM THE STAY	ACTIVITIES I ENJOYED THE MOST

PLACES I WOULD RECOMMEND (RESTAURANTS, SHOPPING, ENTERTAINMENT, ETC.)

SPECIAL MESSAGE TO THE HOST

Guest Book

GUEST NAME	
DATE ARRIVED	
TRAVELING FROM	
WEATHER	

CONTACT NUMBER	
DATE DEPARTED	

MY FAVORITE THING ABOUT THE PROPERTY

MY FAVORITE MEMORY FROM THE STAY | ACTIVITIES I ENJOYED THE MOST

PLACES I WOULD RECOMMEND
(RESTAURANTS, SHOPPING, ENTERTAINMENT, ETC.)

SPECIAL MESSAGE TO THE HOST

Guest Book

GUEST NAME		CONTACT NUMBER	
DATE ARRIVED		DATE DEPARTED	
TRAVELING FROM			
WEATHER			

MY FAVORITE THING ABOUT THE PROPERTY

MY FAVORITE MEMORY FROM THE STAY	ACTIVITIES I ENJOYED THE MOST

| PLACES I WOULD RECOMMEND |
(RESTAURANTS, SHOPPING, ENTERTAINMENT, ETC.)

SPECIAL MESSAGE TO THE HOST

Guest Book

GUEST NAME		CONTACT NUMBER	
DATE ARRIVED		DATE DEPARTED	
TRAVELING FROM			
WEATHER			

MY FAVORITE THING ABOUT THE PROPERTY

MY FAVORITE MEMORY FROM THE STAY	ACTIVITIES I ENJOYED THE MOST

| PLACES I WOULD RECOMMEND |
(RESTAURANTS, SHOPPING, ENTERTAINMENT, ETC.)

SPECIAL MESSAGE TO THE HOST

Guest Book

GUEST NAME	
DATE ARRIVED	
TRAVELING FROM	
WEATHER	

CONTACT NUMBER	
DATE DEPARTED	

MY FAVORITE THING ABOUT THE PROPERTY

MY FAVORITE MEMORY FROM THE STAY	ACTIVITIES I ENJOYED THE MOST

PLACES I WOULD RECOMMEND
(RESTAURANTS, SHOPPING, ENTERTAINMENT, ETC.)

SPECIAL MESSAGE TO THE HOST

Guest Book

GUEST NAME		CONTACT NUMBER	
DATE ARRIVED		DATE DEPARTED	
TRAVELING FROM			
WEATHER			

MY FAVORITE THING ABOUT THE PROPERTY

MY FAVORITE MEMORY FROM THE STAY	ACTIVITIES I ENJOYED THE MOST

PLACES I WOULD RECOMMEND
(RESTAURANTS, SHOPPING, ENTERTAINMENT, ETC.)

SPECIAL MESSAGE TO THE HOST

Guest Book

GUEST NAME		CONTACT NUMBER	
DATE ARRIVED		DATE DEPARTED	
TRAVELING FROM			
WEATHER			

MY FAVORITE THING ABOUT THE PROPERTY

MY FAVORITE MEMORY FROM THE STAY	ACTIVITIES I ENJOYED THE MOST

PLACES I WOULD RECOMMEND
(RESTAURANTS, SHOPPING, ENTERTAINMENT, ETC.)

SPECIAL MESSAGE TO THE HOST

Guest Book

GUEST NAME		CONTACT NUMBER	
DATE ARRIVED		DATE DEPARTED	
TRAVELING FROM			
WEATHER			

MY FAVORITE THING ABOUT THE PROPERTY

MY FAVORITE MEMORY FROM THE STAY	ACTIVITIES I ENJOYED THE MOST

PLACES I WOULD RECOMMEND (RESTAURANTS, SHOPPING, ENTERTAINMENT, ETC.)

SPECIAL MESSAGE TO THE HOST

Guest Book

GUEST NAME		CONTACT NUMBER	
DATE ARRIVED		DATE DEPARTED	
TRAVELING FROM			
WEATHER			

MY FAVORITE THING ABOUT THE PROPERTY

MY FAVORITE MEMORY FROM THE STAY	ACTIVITIES I ENJOYED THE MOST

PLACES I WOULD RECOMMEND (RESTAURANTS, SHOPPING, ENTERTAINMENT, ETC.)

SPECIAL MESSAGE TO THE HOST

Guest Book

GUEST NAME		CONTACT NUMBER	
DATE ARRIVED		DATE DEPARTED	
TRAVELING FROM			
WEATHER			

MY FAVORITE THING ABOUT THE PROPERTY

MY FAVORITE MEMORY FROM THE STAY	ACTIVITIES I ENJOYED THE MOST

PLACES I WOULD RECOMMEND
(RESTAURANTS, SHOPPING, ENTERTAINMENT, ETC.)

SPECIAL MESSAGE TO THE HOST

Guest Book

GUEST NAME		CONTACT NUMBER	
DATE ARRIVED		DATE DEPARTED	
TRAVELING FROM			
WEATHER			

MY FAVORITE THING ABOUT THE PROPERTY

MY FAVORITE MEMORY FROM THE STAY	ACTIVITIES I ENJOYED THE MOST

| PLACES I WOULD RECOMMEND |
(RESTAURANTS, SHOPPING, ENTERTAINMENT, ETC.)

SPECIAL MESSAGE TO THE HOST

Guest Book

GUEST NAME		CONTACT NUMBER	
DATE ARRIVED		DATE DEPARTED	
TRAVELING FROM			
WEATHER			

MY FAVORITE THING ABOUT THE PROPERTY

MY FAVORITE MEMORY FROM THE STAY	ACTIVITIES I ENJOYED THE MOST

PLACES I WOULD RECOMMEND
(RESTAURANTS, SHOPPING, ENTERTAINMENT, ETC.)

SPECIAL MESSAGE TO THE HOST

Guest Book

GUEST NAME		CONTACT NUMBER	
DATE ARRIVED		DATE DEPARTED	
TRAVELING FROM			
WEATHER			

MY FAVORITE THING ABOUT THE PROPERTY

MY FAVORITE MEMORY FROM THE STAY	ACTIVITIES I ENJOYED THE MOST

PLACES I WOULD RECOMMEND (RESTAURANTS, SHOPPING, ENTERTAINMENT, ETC.)

SPECIAL MESSAGE TO THE HOST

Guest Book

GUEST NAME		CONTACT NUMBER	
DATE ARRIVED		DATE DEPARTED	
TRAVELING FROM			
WEATHER			

MY FAVORITE THING ABOUT THE PROPERTY

MY FAVORITE MEMORY FROM THE STAY	ACTIVITIES I ENJOYED THE MOST

PLACES I WOULD RECOMMEND (RESTAURANTS, SHOPPING, ENTERTAINMENT, ETC.)

SPECIAL MESSAGE TO THE HOST

Guest Book

GUEST NAME		CONTACT NUMBER	
DATE ARRIVED		DATE DEPARTED	
TRAVELING FROM			
WEATHER			

MY FAVORITE THING ABOUT THE PROPERTY

MY FAVORITE MEMORY FROM THE STAY	ACTIVITIES I ENJOYED THE MOST

PLACES I WOULD RECOMMEND
(RESTAURANTS, SHOPPING, ENTERTAINMENT, ETC.)

SPECIAL MESSAGE TO THE HOST

Guest Book

GUEST NAME		CONTACT NUMBER	
DATE ARRIVED		DATE DEPARTED	
TRAVELING FROM			
WEATHER			

MY FAVORITE THING ABOUT THE PROPERTY

MY FAVORITE MEMORY FROM THE STAY	ACTIVITIES I ENJOYED THE MOST

| PLACES I WOULD RECOMMEND |
(RESTAURANTS, SHOPPING, ENTERTAINMENT, ETC.)

SPECIAL MESSAGE TO THE HOST

Guest Book

GUEST NAME		CONTACT NUMBER	
DATE ARRIVED		DATE DEPARTED	
TRAVELING FROM			
WEATHER			

MY FAVORITE THING ABOUT THE PROPERTY

MY FAVORITE MEMORY FROM THE STAY	ACTIVITIES I ENJOYED THE MOST

| PLACES I WOULD RECOMMEND |
(RESTAURANTS, SHOPPING, ENTERTAINMENT, ETC.)

SPECIAL MESSAGE TO THE HOST

Guest Book

GUEST NAME		CONTACT NUMBER	
DATE ARRIVED		DATE DEPARTED	
TRAVELING FROM			
WEATHER			

MY FAVORITE THING ABOUT THE PROPERTY

MY FAVORITE MEMORY FROM THE STAY	ACTIVITIES I ENJOYED THE MOST

| PLACES I WOULD RECOMMEND |
(RESTAURANTS, SHOPPING, ENTERTAINMENT, ETC.)

SPECIAL MESSAGE TO THE HOST

Guest Book

GUEST NAME		CONTACT NUMBER	
DATE ARRIVED		DATE DEPARTED	
TRAVELING FROM			
WEATHER			

MY FAVORITE THING ABOUT THE PROPERTY

MY FAVORITE MEMORY FROM THE STAY	ACTIVITIES I ENJOYED THE MOST

PLACES I WOULD RECOMMEND
(RESTAURANTS, SHOPPING, ENTERTAINMENT, ETC.)

SPECIAL MESSAGE TO THE HOST

Guest Book

GUEST NAME		CONTACT NUMBER	
DATE ARRIVED		DATE DEPARTED	
TRAVELING FROM			
WEATHER			

MY FAVORITE THING ABOUT THE PROPERTY

MY FAVORITE MEMORY FROM THE STAY	ACTIVITIES I ENJOYED THE MOST

| PLACES I WOULD RECOMMEND |
(RESTAURANTS, SHOPPING, ENTERTAINMENT, ETC.)

SPECIAL MESSAGE TO THE HOST

Guest Book

GUEST NAME		CONTACT NUMBER	
DATE ARRIVED		DATE DEPARTED	
TRAVELING FROM			
WEATHER			

MY FAVORITE THING ABOUT THE PROPERTY

MY FAVORITE MEMORY FROM THE STAY	ACTIVITIES I ENJOYED THE MOST

PLACES I WOULD RECOMMEND
(RESTAURANTS, SHOPPING, ENTERTAINMENT, ETC.)

SPECIAL MESSAGE TO THE HOST

Guest Book

GUEST NAME		CONTACT NUMBER	
DATE ARRIVED		DATE DEPARTED	
TRAVELING FROM			
WEATHER			

MY FAVORITE THING ABOUT THE PROPERTY

MY FAVORITE MEMORY FROM THE STAY	ACTIVITIES I ENJOYED THE MOST

PLACES I WOULD RECOMMEND
(RESTAURANTS, SHOPPING, ENTERTAINMENT, ETC.)

SPECIAL MESSAGE TO THE HOST

Guest Book

GUEST NAME		CONTACT NUMBER	
DATE ARRIVED		DATE DEPARTED	
TRAVELING FROM			
WEATHER			

MY FAVORITE THING ABOUT THE PROPERTY

MY FAVORITE MEMORY FROM THE STAY	ACTIVITIES I ENJOYED THE MOST

PLACES I WOULD RECOMMEND (RESTAURANTS, SHOPPING, ENTERTAINMENT, ETC.)

SPECIAL MESSAGE TO THE HOST

Guest Book

GUEST NAME		CONTACT NUMBER	
DATE ARRIVED		DATE DEPARTED	
TRAVELING FROM			
WEATHER			

MY FAVORITE THING ABOUT THE PROPERTY

MY FAVORITE MEMORY FROM THE STAY	ACTIVITIES I ENJOYED THE MOST

PLACES I WOULD RECOMMEND
(RESTAURANTS, SHOPPING, ENTERTAINMENT, ETC.)

SPECIAL MESSAGE TO THE HOST

Guest Book

GUEST NAME		CONTACT NUMBER	
DATE ARRIVED		DATE DEPARTED	
TRAVELING FROM			
WEATHER			

MY FAVORITE THING ABOUT THE PROPERTY

MY FAVORITE MEMORY FROM THE STAY	ACTIVITIES I ENJOYED THE MOST

PLACES I WOULD RECOMMEND (RESTAURANTS, SHOPPING, ENTERTAINMENT, ETC.)

SPECIAL MESSAGE TO THE HOST

Guest Book

GUEST NAME		CONTACT NUMBER	
DATE ARRIVED		DATE DEPARTED	
TRAVELING FROM			
WEATHER			

MY FAVORITE THING ABOUT THE PROPERTY

MY FAVORITE MEMORY FROM THE STAY	ACTIVITIES I ENJOYED THE MOST

PLACES I WOULD RECOMMEND (RESTAURANTS, SHOPPING, ENTERTAINMENT, ETC.)

SPECIAL MESSAGE TO THE HOST

Guest Book

GUEST NAME		CONTACT NUMBER	
DATE ARRIVED		DATE DEPARTED	
TRAVELING FROM			
WEATHER			

MY FAVORITE THING ABOUT THE PROPERTY

MY FAVORITE MEMORY FROM THE STAY	ACTIVITIES I ENJOYED THE MOST

PLACES I WOULD RECOMMEND
(RESTAURANTS, SHOPPING, ENTERTAINMENT, ETC.)

SPECIAL MESSAGE TO THE HOST

Guest Book

GUEST NAME		CONTACT NUMBER	
DATE ARRIVED		DATE DEPARTED	
TRAVELING FROM			
WEATHER			

MY FAVORITE THING ABOUT THE PROPERTY

MY FAVORITE MEMORY FROM THE STAY	ACTIVITIES I ENJOYED THE MOST

| PLACES I WOULD RECOMMEND |
(RESTAURANTS, SHOPPING, ENTERTAINMENT, ETC.)

SPECIAL MESSAGE TO THE HOST

Guest Book

GUEST NAME		CONTACT NUMBER	
DATE ARRIVED		DATE DEPARTED	
TRAVELING FROM			
WEATHER			

MY FAVORITE THING ABOUT THE PROPERTY

MY FAVORITE MEMORY FROM THE STAY	ACTIVITIES I ENJOYED THE MOST

PLACES I WOULD RECOMMEND (RESTAURANTS, SHOPPING, ENTERTAINMENT, ETC.)

SPECIAL MESSAGE TO THE HOST

Guest Book

GUEST NAME		CONTACT NUMBER	
DATE ARRIVED		DATE DEPARTED	
TRAVELING FROM			
WEATHER			

MY FAVORITE THING ABOUT THE PROPERTY

MY FAVORITE MEMORY FROM THE STAY	ACTIVITIES I ENJOYED THE MOST

PLACES I WOULD RECOMMEND
(RESTAURANTS, SHOPPING, ENTERTAINMENT, ETC.)

SPECIAL MESSAGE TO THE HOST

Guest Book

GUEST NAME		CONTACT NUMBER	
DATE ARRIVED		DATE DEPARTED	
TRAVELING FROM			
WEATHER			

MY FAVORITE THING ABOUT THE PROPERTY

MY FAVORITE MEMORY FROM THE STAY	ACTIVITIES I ENJOYED THE MOST

| PLACES I WOULD RECOMMEND |
(RESTAURANTS, SHOPPING, ENTERTAINMENT, ETC.)

SPECIAL MESSAGE TO THE HOST

Guest Book

GUEST NAME		CONTACT NUMBER	
DATE ARRIVED		DATE DEPARTED	
TRAVELING FROM			
WEATHER			

MY FAVORITE THING ABOUT THE PROPERTY

MY FAVORITE MEMORY FROM THE STAY	ACTIVITIES I ENJOYED THE MOST

| PLACES I WOULD RECOMMEND |
(RESTAURANTS, SHOPPING, ENTERTAINMENT, ETC.)

SPECIAL MESSAGE TO THE HOST

Guest Book

GUEST NAME		CONTACT NUMBER	
DATE ARRIVED		DATE DEPARTED	
TRAVELING FROM			
WEATHER			

MY FAVORITE THING ABOUT THE PROPERTY

MY FAVORITE MEMORY FROM THE STAY	ACTIVITIES I ENJOYED THE MOST

| PLACES I WOULD RECOMMEND |
(RESTAURANTS, SHOPPING, ENTERTAINMENT, ETC.)

SPECIAL MESSAGE TO THE HOST

Guest Book

GUEST NAME		CONTACT NUMBER	
DATE ARRIVED		DATE DEPARTED	
TRAVELING FROM			
WEATHER			

MY FAVORITE THING ABOUT THE PROPERTY

MY FAVORITE MEMORY FROM THE STAY	ACTIVITIES I ENJOYED THE MOST

PLACES I WOULD RECOMMEND
(RESTAURANTS, SHOPPING, ENTERTAINMENT, ETC.)

SPECIAL MESSAGE TO THE HOST

Guest Book

GUEST NAME		CONTACT NUMBER	
DATE ARRIVED		DATE DEPARTED	
TRAVELING FROM			
WEATHER			

MY FAVORITE THING ABOUT THE PROPERTY

MY FAVORITE MEMORY FROM THE STAY	ACTIVITIES I ENJOYED THE MOST

PLACES I WOULD RECOMMEND (RESTAURANTS, SHOPPING, ENTERTAINMENT, ETC.)

SPECIAL MESSAGE TO THE HOST

Guest Book

GUEST NAME		CONTACT NUMBER	
DATE ARRIVED		DATE DEPARTED	
TRAVELING FROM			
WEATHER			

MY FAVORITE THING ABOUT THE PROPERTY

MY FAVORITE MEMORY FROM THE STAY	ACTIVITIES I ENJOYED THE MOST

PLACES I WOULD RECOMMEND
(RESTAURANTS, SHOPPING, ENTERTAINMENT, ETC.)

SPECIAL MESSAGE TO THE HOST

Guest Book

GUEST NAME		CONTACT NUMBER	
DATE ARRIVED		DATE DEPARTED	
TRAVELING FROM			
WEATHER			

MY FAVORITE THING ABOUT THE PROPERTY

MY FAVORITE MEMORY FROM THE STAY	ACTIVITIES I ENJOYED THE MOST

PLACES I WOULD RECOMMEND
(RESTAURANTS, SHOPPING, ENTERTAINMENT, ETC.)

SPECIAL MESSAGE TO THE HOST

Guest Book

GUEST NAME		CONTACT NUMBER	
DATE ARRIVED		DATE DEPARTED	
TRAVELING FROM			
WEATHER			

MY FAVORITE THING ABOUT THE PROPERTY

MY FAVORITE MEMORY FROM THE STAY	ACTIVITIES I ENJOYED THE MOST

PLACES I WOULD RECOMMEND
(RESTAURANTS, SHOPPING, ENTERTAINMENT, ETC.)

SPECIAL MESSAGE TO THE HOST

Guest Book

GUEST NAME		CONTACT NUMBER	
DATE ARRIVED		DATE DEPARTED	
TRAVELING FROM			
WEATHER			

MY FAVORITE THING ABOUT THE PROPERTY

MY FAVORITE MEMORY FROM THE STAY	ACTIVITIES I ENJOYED THE MOST

PLACES I WOULD RECOMMEND (RESTAURANTS, SHOPPING, ENTERTAINMENT, ETC.)

SPECIAL MESSAGE TO THE HOST

Guest Book

GUEST NAME		CONTACT NUMBER	
DATE ARRIVED		DATE DEPARTED	
TRAVELING FROM			
WEATHER			

MY FAVORITE THING ABOUT THE PROPERTY

MY FAVORITE MEMORY FROM THE STAY	ACTIVITIES I ENJOYED THE MOST

| PLACES I WOULD RECOMMEND |
(RESTAURANTS, SHOPPING, ENTERTAINMENT, ETC.)

SPECIAL MESSAGE TO THE HOST

Guest Book

GUEST NAME		CONTACT NUMBER	
DATE ARRIVED		DATE DEPARTED	
TRAVELING FROM			
WEATHER			

MY FAVORITE THING ABOUT THE PROPERTY

MY FAVORITE MEMORY FROM THE STAY	ACTIVITIES I ENJOYED THE MOST

PLACES I WOULD RECOMMEND (RESTAURANTS, SHOPPING, ENTERTAINMENT, ETC.)

SPECIAL MESSAGE TO THE HOST

Guest Book

GUEST NAME		CONTACT NUMBER	
DATE ARRIVED		DATE DEPARTED	
TRAVELING FROM			
WEATHER			

MY FAVORITE THING ABOUT THE PROPERTY

MY FAVORITE MEMORY FROM THE STAY	ACTIVITIES I ENJOYED THE MOST

PLACES I WOULD RECOMMEND
(RESTAURANTS, SHOPPING, ENTERTAINMENT, ETC.)

SPECIAL MESSAGE TO THE HOST

Guest Book

GUEST NAME		CONTACT NUMBER	
DATE ARRIVED		DATE DEPARTED	
TRAVELING FROM			
WEATHER			

MY FAVORITE THING ABOUT THE PROPERTY

MY FAVORITE MEMORY FROM THE STAY	ACTIVITIES I ENJOYED THE MOST

| PLACES I WOULD RECOMMEND |
(RESTAURANTS, SHOPPING, ENTERTAINMENT, ETC.)

SPECIAL MESSAGE TO THE HOST

Guest Book

GUEST NAME		CONTACT NUMBER	
DATE ARRIVED		DATE DEPARTED	
TRAVELING FROM			
WEATHER			

MY FAVORITE THING ABOUT THE PROPERTY

MY FAVORITE MEMORY FROM THE STAY	ACTIVITIES I ENJOYED THE MOST

| PLACES I WOULD RECOMMEND |
(RESTAURANTS, SHOPPING, ENTERTAINMENT, ETC.)

SPECIAL MESSAGE TO THE HOST

Guest Book

GUEST NAME		CONTACT NUMBER	
DATE ARRIVED		DATE DEPARTED	
TRAVELING FROM			
WEATHER			

MY FAVORITE THING ABOUT THE PROPERTY

MY FAVORITE MEMORY FROM THE STAY	ACTIVITIES I ENJOYED THE MOST

PLACES I WOULD RECOMMEND (RESTAURANTS, SHOPPING, ENTERTAINMENT, ETC.)

SPECIAL MESSAGE TO THE HOST

Guest Book

GUEST NAME		CONTACT NUMBER	
DATE ARRIVED		DATE DEPARTED	
TRAVELING FROM			
WEATHER			

MY FAVORITE THING ABOUT THE PROPERTY

MY FAVORITE MEMORY FROM THE STAY	ACTIVITIES I ENJOYED THE MOST

| PLACES I WOULD RECOMMEND |
(RESTAURANTS, SHOPPING, ENTERTAINMENT, ETC.)

SPECIAL MESSAGE TO THE HOST

Guest Book

GUEST NAME		CONTACT NUMBER	
DATE ARRIVED		DATE DEPARTED	
TRAVELING FROM			
WEATHER			

MY FAVORITE THING ABOUT THE PROPERTY

MY FAVORITE MEMORY FROM THE STAY	ACTIVITIES I ENJOYED THE MOST

| PLACES I WOULD RECOMMEND |
(RESTAURANTS, SHOPPING, ENTERTAINMENT, ETC.)

SPECIAL MESSAGE TO THE HOST

Guest Book

GUEST NAME		CONTACT NUMBER	
DATE ARRIVED		DATE DEPARTED	
TRAVELING FROM			
WEATHER			

MY FAVORITE THING ABOUT THE PROPERTY

MY FAVORITE MEMORY FROM THE STAY	ACTIVITIES I ENJOYED THE MOST

| PLACES I WOULD RECOMMEND |
(RESTAURANTS, SHOPPING, ENTERTAINMENT, ETC.)

SPECIAL MESSAGE TO THE HOST

Guest Book

GUEST NAME		CONTACT NUMBER	
DATE ARRIVED		DATE DEPARTED	
TRAVELING FROM			
WEATHER			

MY FAVORITE THING ABOUT THE PROPERTY

MY FAVORITE MEMORY FROM THE STAY	ACTIVITIES I ENJOYED THE MOST

| PLACES I WOULD RECOMMEND |
(RESTAURANTS, SHOPPING, ENTERTAINMENT, ETC.)

SPECIAL MESSAGE TO THE HOST

Guest Book

GUEST NAME		CONTACT NUMBER	
DATE ARRIVED		DATE DEPARTED	
TRAVELING FROM			
WEATHER			

MY FAVORITE THING ABOUT THE PROPERTY

MY FAVORITE MEMORY FROM THE STAY	ACTIVITIES I ENJOYED THE MOST

PLACES I WOULD RECOMMEND (RESTAURANTS, SHOPPING, ENTERTAINMENT, ETC.)

SPECIAL MESSAGE TO THE HOST

Guest Book

GUEST NAME		CONTACT NUMBER	
DATE ARRIVED		DATE DEPARTED	
TRAVELING FROM			
WEATHER			

MY FAVORITE THING ABOUT THE PROPERTY

MY FAVORITE MEMORY FROM THE STAY	ACTIVITIES I ENJOYED THE MOST

PLACES I WOULD RECOMMEND (RESTAURANTS, SHOPPING, ENTERTAINMENT, ETC.)

SPECIAL MESSAGE TO THE HOST

Guest Book

GUEST NAME		CONTACT NUMBER	
DATE ARRIVED		DATE DEPARTED	
TRAVELING FROM			
WEATHER			

MY FAVORITE THING ABOUT THE PROPERTY

MY FAVORITE MEMORY FROM THE STAY	ACTIVITIES I ENJOYED THE MOST

PLACES I WOULD RECOMMEND
(RESTAURANTS, SHOPPING, ENTERTAINMENT, ETC.)

SPECIAL MESSAGE TO THE HOST